BRITISH ACHIEVEMEN

CIVILIAN SUPPLIES IN WARTIME BRITAIN

In response to requests for an account of British wartime developments and institutions, the British Ministry of Information has had this series of booklets specially prepared. The Ministry believes the treatment of the subject to be fair and adequate within the space available, but any opinions expressed are in each instance those of the author.

EMERGENCY FEEDING *A mobile canteen serves hot drinks to bombed-out people in the East End of London. It is the morning after a raid in the blitz of 1940–41.*

CIVILIAN SUPPLIES IN WARTIME BRITAIN

by

MONICA FELTON

Published by

THE MINISTRY OF INFORMATION · LONDON

Printed in England

CONTENTS

CIVILIAN SUPPLIES IN WARTIME BRITAIN

CHAPTER I

Introduction

LOOKING BACKWARDS is a common and not unprofitable form of day-dreaming. But after nearly six years of war, memories of the details of everyday life in 1939 are apt to become a little blurred. A scene flashed on to the screen of a cinema may show Piccadilly Circus at midnight, with neon lights illuminating brilliant advertisements of whisky and tonic-water, chewing-gum and cigarettes. The Circus itself is crowded, an immense and shining traffic jam in which buses and taxis and private cars are wedged tightly, apparently immovable, around the statue of Eros at the centre, while pedestrians stand at the pavement's edge or scurry into the Tube station below. The 1945 audience watches, gasping. They remember when Eros was taken down to be removed to a place of safety in the country, out of reach of bombs, but they find it difficult to recall that the lights were ever as bright as those shining down from the screen in front of them, or that the traffic was ever so dense or evenings in the centre of London ever so long and so gay.

Or an old newspaper tumbles out of a forgotten corner and the housewife picks it up, astonished first at its bulk, three or four times the size of this morning's paper in which news from all the world is crammed into four meagre pages. She opens it, and, characteristically, looks first at the advertisements: the fashions, lavishly illustrated, have the odd dowdy appearance typical of the recently out-of-date—but they look fussy, too, the dresses, coats and undergarments elaborately frilled and tucked and flared, an ugly contrast with the simple lines of wartime austerity fashions. The prices, she notices, are generally lower than those of the garments on which she is planning to spend her next allocation of clothing coupons—but not as much lower as her imperfect memory and her knowledge of the wartime purchase tax had led her to imagine—and then she remembers that purchase tax is not payable on utility clothes and that the Board of Trade's Utility Scheme has not only raised the standard of design of clothes bought by women of moderate means but has resulted in a reduction in the price of many articles from the levels reached in 1940.

She turns over the pages and envy rises again as she glances at more advertisements : cosmetics, heavily perfumed and elaborately packed, canned goods, breakfast foods, chocolates and confectionery, biscuits, jellies and ice-cream mixtures in bewildering variety, vacuum cleaners, radio sets, household linen and china, and, last of all, well displayed advice to " Eat More Bread " or " Eat More Fruit ". But this last injunction is perhaps the only one that really hurts. Except in fruit-growing districts, the combined effects of indifferent crops, the need to conserve soft fruits for the manufacture of jam, and the shortage of shipping which has restricted imports to articles of real necessity have meant that most families have been lucky to taste strawberries or other soft fruits more than once or twice a year. With this exception she finds, most astonishingly of all, how easily she has learned to do without all sorts of things that she once regarded as necessities and how few things that are really necessary she has in fact had to sacrifice.

There have been shortages and hardships, but they are less severe than most people in 1939, had they visualised a long war, would have dared to anticipate, and far fewer than men and women with clear memories of the war of 1914–18 could have believed possible. To-day the most acute shortage is of house-room, both in London and other heavily bombed areas, and in those districts where the growth of munitions industries was accompanied by a large influx of population. There is a shortage of fuel, but though many families have had to make drastic cuts in their consumption of coal, gas and electricity, few have been obliged to do without a necessary fire. Household goods of all kinds have become worn and shabby and breakages are difficult to replace, but even in 1944 it was still possible for one person in three to buy a new kettle, saucepan or frying-pan in the course of the year and one person in four a teapot or jug. The clothing ration to-day allows the consumer about half the quantity he bought before the war : and the ration is honoured—with few exceptions supply is maintained at a level high enough to meet this limited demand, and when, as sometimes happens, a sudden shortage develops, it is usually overcome with reasonable, and sometimes surprising, speed.

Food, though not always plentiful, has never been less than adequate. If it has sometimes been lacking in interest and variety, it has been invariably wholesome and well balanced in its content of essential vitamins and minerals. Indeed, wartime organisation of the supply and distribution of food has secured a marked rise in the nutritional standards of the poorest sections of the population—a rise due not only to the virtual abolition of unemployment but also to the adoption of a food policy which has included, in addition to rationing, subsidising of the prices of essential foodstuffs, the education of the public in the science of food values, and the distribution of foods with high protective qualities, such as milk, orange-juice and cod-liver oil, in accordance with the needs rather than the means of the recipients.

The average consumer, and particularly the average housewife, may have only a hazy idea of the means by which she is enabled to buy most of her essential needs at prices which she can afford. But she is very conscious of the magnitude of this achievement. She has almost certainly not read of the White Paper on *Statistics Relating to the War Effort of the United Kingdom*, but the day-to-day evidence of her own eyes makes it clear that the drive for production never failed to put the needs of the Armed Forces first. The woman in the home has had to make-do with whatever could be spared, but wise planning has ensured that although she has rarely, since 1940, enjoyed plenty, she has seldom had less than enough. Now and then she grumbles, but not often and not for long. She is generous with praise and a complaint about some specific and immediate shortage is usually followed by the observation that we in this country have, on the whole, been extraordinarily lucky.

Luck is not, of course, the explanation. The satisfaction of consumers' needs was recognised, by those responsible for the war effort as a whole, as an essential part of the total programme. The grand strategy recognised the importance of the Home Front and careful planning was necessary to ensure that sacrifices should not be demanded unnecessarily and that where they had to be made the resulting hardships should be cut to the minimum.

The policy thus formulated has been carried out in a long series of measures, some requiring legislation and others through administrative action, that have been both complex and flexible. Imports have been reduced by 60 per cent. since 1939 ; home production of food has been rapidly increased ; factories manufacturing articles for civilian consumption were switched to munitions production or closed down altogether ; such consumption goods as are still made are standardised, limited in quantity and, for the most part, sold at fixed prices. Rationing has been extended to cover not only food and clothing but furniture, chocolate, confectionery and soap. Sometimes, as with clothes rationing, changes have been introduced suddenly ; sometimes, as with the concentration of production, lengthy consultation with all the interests concerned has preceded action. But always, without a single exception, the spirit as well as the form of democracy has been kept vigorously alive. As significant as questions and debates in Parliament are the hundreds of local organisations in every part of the country which act as channels for public criticism and serve to control many of the day-to-day details of nationally agreed policy. Local authorities, local food control committees and other bodies are in close touch with opinion in the areas they serve, and their membership is made up of representative citizens with direct personal experience of the problems with which they are called upon to deal, whether it be the provision of a communal meals service, the hours at which shops may be opened, rationing, salvage, or one of a hundred other small but important problems.

Democratic control has, too, proved remarkably flexible. Indeed, a lively barrage of public criticism has enabled mistakes to be recognised—and remedied—quickly. In the chapters that follow an attempt is made to trace the history of the main types of restriction on the consumers' freedom of choice—limitation of supplies, control over the production of consumers' goods, price control, "austerity" regulations and rationing—from the outbreak of war to the end of 1944. The general trend has been, inevitably, in the direction of an increasing stringency coupled with a steady increase in the productive efficiency of both farmers and manufacturers: and the ordinary citizen, working harder and for longer hours than ever before, has endured willingly, with a willingness that has flowed from a common understanding of the part that these restrictions have played in making possible the victorious conclusion of the war.

CHAPTER II

The Problems of Production

Organisation at the Centre

WHEN THE WAR broke out the Ministry of Supply had already been set up to undertake responsibility for the production of munitions and stores for the Army; later this Ministry was also made responsible for the control of most raw materials. The Air Ministry remained responsible for all supplies to the Royal Air

Force until May 1940, when the Ministry of Aircraft Production was created; and the Admiralty was, and has remained, responsible for the supply of naval equipment of all kinds (and also, since February 1940, for Merchant Shipbuilding). Similarly, the duty of ensuring the maintenance of supplies adequate to meet the essential needs of the civilian population was divided between several Government departments. The peacetime duties of the Ministry of Agriculture and Fisheries had to be extended in various directions as the need to increase home production grew more acute. A Ministry of Food was set up within a few days of the outbreak of war to ensure the maintenance of food supplies and to organise distribution. Control over the production of most consumers' goods other than food rested with the Board of Trade, though the quantities of raw materials allocated for use in the manufacture of these goods was determined in consultation with the Raw Materials Department of the Ministry of Supply. The Ministry of Supply is also responsible for the salvaging of waste products of all kinds, a task which, as far as domestic salvage is concerned, has been carried out with the aid of helpers organised by Women's Voluntary Services. A wide range of duties in connection with the organisation of the coal industry, the gas and electricity industries, and the importation and sale of petroleum products are undertaken by the Ministry of Fuel and Power. The Ministry of Production, set up in February 1942, is mainly a co-ordinating department.

Each of these departments has been staffed by both permanent and temporary civil servants, and while there have been among the former men and women with a wide experience of the problems of public administration, the latter have included experts with previous business experience or academic knowledge of the subjects they have been called upon to handle. Major changes in the powers and duties of the different departments are embodied in legislation passed by Parliament; changes of a minor character—such as the issue of regulations within a generally approved framework—are made by Orders in Council which Parliament can, if it so pleases, annul. Public criticism of the work of departments is voiced regularly on the floor of the House of Commons in questions to the Ministers concerned, as well as in debates on the appropriate occasions, and Members of Parliament have exercised considerable vigilance to ensure that the enormous volume of wartime regulations that govern civilian life should be subject to all the processes of democratic control.

In addition to its headquarters organisation, each department has a regional organisation, in some though not all cases corresponding to the regions into which the country was divided for purposes of civil defence. Regional organisations are responsible for much of the day-to-day administration of the different departments and have a close and direct contact with producers and consumers.

Agricultural Production and Imported Foodstuffs

The maintenance of food supplies has been since the outbreak of war the joint responsibility of the Ministry of Food and the Ministry of Agriculture, since while the former is charged with the task of providing a diet that is physiologically adequate, it is the duty of the latter to organise domestic food production to meet the largest possible proportion of domestic needs. In practice, this means that plans have to be made something like eighteen months ahead : the Ministry of Food makes an estimate of the nutritional needs of the population in terms of calories, proteins, fats and minerals ; the volume of production that can be expected from domestic agriculture is then calculated, and the remaining requirements are next translated into terms of available imports. Such a programme has had necessarily to be flexible enough to be adapted to changes in requirements brought about by changes in the war situation, and changes in the supply position, both of imported products and domestic supplies.

A long chapter would be required to describe, even in outline, the contribution that British agriculture has made towards the maintenance of the nation's health, and the way in which this contribution has been achieved. Many thousands of acres of hitherto waste land have been brought under the plough, pasture has been converted to tillage, and land and hot-houses formerly used for the production of flowers and of luxury or out-of-season crops are now growing food of high nutritional value. Milk consumption, in spite of the ploughing-up of grassland and the shortage of imported feeding-stuffs, has increased since 1938, the peak year for dairy-farmers. Land under wheat has increased by over 82 per cent. in England and Wales, and all cereal crops by more than 86·2 per cent. and potatoes by more than 116 per cent. These achievements are all the more remarkable in view of the inevitable decline in the number of workers employed on the land ; they have been brought about not merely by goodwill and enthusiasm, but by a complex, though orderly, policy, which has included financial aid to farmers, price control of all the main products, control of farming operations by local War County Agricultural Committees, representative of both farmers and farm workers, and by an increase in the use of agricultural machinery which has made British farming the most highly mechanised in Europe.

Before the war Britain was dependent on imports for 92 per cent. of her requirements of fat, for 51 per cent. of her meat and bacon, 73 per cent. of her sugar and 87 per cent. of flour cereals, as well as for a large proportion of the cheese, eggs, vegetables and other everyday foods consumed at home. Figures such as these make it plain that while home production was of fundamental importance it could not in any circumstances meet the whole of the nation's requirements. To meet the balance, the Ministry of Food has undertaken the ultimate control of all imported food products, and practically all imports have been either purchased direct for the Ministry or—until August 1945—obtained under Lend-Lease arrangements. On the other hand, though all home-grown foods are handled by traders in accordance with instructions laid down by the Ministry, many of them never pass into Ministry ownership, and the general policy, whether or not the Ministry is at some stage the owner of a particular commodity, is to use the ordinary trade channels of distribution as far as possible. The extent of the Ministry's control varies widely, from meat, where both home-produced and imported supplies are Government property until they reach the retail butcher (though their distribution is handled by traders acting on behalf of the Ministry), to fresh fish, which at no time passes into Ministry ownership; again, with other commodities, of which wheat is an example, imports enter the country as Ministry property, while home-grown supplies remain in private hands.

This control has been accomplished by a carefully planned "concentration" of imports, in order to carry the maximum of food value in every cubic foot of space. Fresh and canned fruit were early eliminated from the import programme on account of their bulkiness; much meat is now imported boneless and in "telescoped" form. Dehydrated foods are playing an increasingly important part. Dried eggs and dried skimmed milk are now accepted by the housewife as regular ingredients of the family meals, and dehydrated meat is, after some trial experiments, now coming into use. These dehydrated foods have the double advantage of saving refrigerator accommodation as well as reducing the total amount of shipping space required.

Manufactured Foodstuffs

Before the war a high, and growing, proportion of the British housewife's food budget was expended on manufactured foods of all kinds: bread, cakes and biscuits; canned meat, fish, fruit and vegetables; prepared breakfast cereals; jellies, sauces, cake and pudding mixtures, and an innumerable variety of other branded goods in packets, cans, jars and bottles. The requirements of the war effort demanded not merely a reduction in the supply of such of these goods as were imported, or whose main ingredients came from abroad, but also a reduction in the number of workers employed in food-processing and packing in this country. At the same time it was necessary to ensure that at a time when the general diet was increasingly lacking in variety such food as continued to be manufactured should be of the highest possible standard of purity and of the maximum nutritional value.

The biggest problem was that of bread, which accounts for 20 per cent. of the weight of food consumed in the United Kingdom and which, together with potatoes, remained unrationed throughout the war, unlike the other basic foodstuffs. Before the war white bread, which was eaten by almost everybody, was made from flour from which all the bran and most of the wheat germ (which contains most of the Vitamin B and iron present in wheat) had been extracted. The deterioration of the shipping situation during 1940 made it desirable to increase as far as possible the percentage of flour extracted in milling and, at the same time, the nutritional value of the loaf, and in March 1941 a National Wheatmeal Loaf was put on the market, made of flour of 85 per cent. extraction instead of the normal 73 per cent. In spite of much propaganda the loaf was not widely popular and many bakers did not find it worth while to make it. The Ministry of Food, anxious not to impose by compulsion an innovation which most people were unwilling to accept, initiated experiments in the " fortification " of the ordinary white loaf by the addition of vitamin B_1. By 1942, however, the continued worsening of the shipping position made it necessary to prohibit the milling of flour of less than 85 per cent. extraction. The loaf has, in fact, been well accepted, and while there have been a few complaints a number of people express a preference for the " National Loaf " now that pre-war white bread has become no more than a memory. This measure, which has contributed substantially to the maintenance of the Nation's health, has released 600,000 tons of shipping for other purposes. For a period it was necessary to conserve shipping space still further by the addition of a small proportion of home-grown rye, oats and barley to the loaf, but these admixtures are now no longer necessary. The loaf is now composed of flour of 80 per cent. extraction which, however, still retains the greater part of the vitamin and mineral content of the wheat.

Margarine is another manufactured foodstuff which ranks high in Britain's wartime diet, though before the war it was eaten only by those who could not afford butter. It was, however, realised from the lessons of 1914–18 that in war conditions it would be difficult to maintain butter supplies of which 90 per cent. are normally imported. After the Munich crisis the Government took the precaution of purchasing large quantities of whale oil, which were stored as a reserve for margarine manufacture. As a result, it was possible to ignore the speculative rise in the price of animal fats that took place in American markets on the outbreak of war and to defer purchasing until prices had fallen once more. Early in 1940 the Ministry of Food took steps to secure that all margarine should contain enough added vitamins A and D to bring it approximately to the level of summer butter, and as a result a full supply of vitaminised margarine was ready to go on the market when Denmark was invaded and its shipments of butter ceased.

Later, the Ministry of Food initiated a scheme for the rationalisation of the margarine and cooking fats industry with the main purpose of economising in transport. As long as margarine was being produced under different brand-names a brand produced in London could be sold in Scotland, and vice versa. Under the new scheme each factory produced the same grades and was allotted a distribution zone designed to reduce transport to the minimum. At the same time, the production of uniform grades, sold at controlled prices, meant that in the event of a factory being damaged by air raids supplies could be diverted from other areas without the complications which would arise from variations in quality and flavour. The scheme has worked well and, in spite of the loss of raw materials from Malaya and the Pacific, the standard of quality has remained high.

The manufacture of most other processed foods has been limited by concentration schemes, designed to release labour in those areas in which the need for workers in munitions production was greatest, and by zoning schemes similar to that used in the distribution of margarine.

The Ministry of Food control the quality of various manufactured foodstuffs and protect the consumer against the excessive claims made by the more unscrupulous type of manufacturer. During 1941, the shortage of such foods as eggs, onions and milk led to the appearance on the market of substitutes, some of which were of only limited value while others were no better than expensive frauds. As a result, the Food Substitutes Order was introduced on October 11, 1941, prohibiting the sale of any food substitute except under licence from the Ministry of Food. The Food Standards (General Provisions) Order and the Labelling of Food Order, both issued in 1944 under the Defence (Sale of Food) Regulations, gave the Minister of Food power to regulate the composition, labelling and advertising of food, and made it an offence to issue false labels and advertisements, particularly with regard to the nutritional and dietary value of foods. In these and other ways wartime control over food manufacture was accompanied by a steadily increasing measure of protection for the consumer as well, as will be seen later, as of measures designed to increase his—or rather her—knowledge of food values and dietary problems. The total saving of transport and of labour effected by these schemes has been very large indeed, and consumers, though missing their favourite brands, are often heard to express a gratified astonishment at the range of variety that remains.

Clothing and Household Goods

On the outbreak of war, control over the supply of goods for civilian consumption was exercised only through control over the raw materials of industry, and the Board of Trade's first direct cut in the supply of consumer goods for the home market was not made until April 1940. At that time the capacity of the cotton industry was being severely strained to meet Government orders and the needs of the export trade, and the Cotton, Linen and Rayon Order was introduced with the object of reducing supplies to the general public by limiting the quantities which retailers were permitted to purchase. This was followed in June 1940 by the Limitation of Supplies (Miscellaneous) Order, under which manufacturers and wholesalers were forbidden to sell to retailers in the home market goods in excess of two-thirds of the value of those sold during the six months June–December 1939. The Order was revised in December 1940 with the object of cutting supplies still further: the sale of the more essential goods was reduced to half the value of similar goods sold during the standard period, while the sale of less essential goods was restricted to a quarter of normal consumption.

These measures were designed both to conserve stocks and to release labour, raw materials and factory space for more essential purposes, and in the period from June 1940 to April 1941 the number of workers engaged in the industries covered by the Orders fell by about 60 per cent. But this success, though statistically impressive, was of a rough and ready character. Cuts in output were of the same magnitude for all firms, wherever they were situated. Hence, the Orders achieved less than might have been hoped for in the areas where munitions production was most concentrated and where the need for labour and additional space was most acute, while in other areas workers were sometimes thrown out of work or employed only part-time, and of course large numbers of factories were operating well below capacity. It was in the light of the difficulties thus created that the Government in March 1941 announced the decision to introduce measures for the concentration of production into the smallest possible number of factories, each of which would operate full-time.

Concentration of Production

Some seventy industries were covered by concentration schemes, and though the details varied with varying circumstances, the general principles followed were similar in each case. When it was decided that an industry was suitable for concentration, officers of the Board of Trade discussed the broad questions of policy involved with a gathering of representatives of the employers and workers concerned, and the industry was informed of the areas in which it was chiefly desired that firms should be closed and the percentage of labour which it was aimed to release. The industry was then invited to devise its own scheme, with the proviso that if the firms concerned failed to come to an agreement within a reasonable time it would be necessary for a scheme to be imposed compulsorily. Each completed scheme was based on the division of all firms in an industry into two main categories: "Nucleus firms", which were allowed to continue in operation and were given some measure of protection for their labour and some priority in the supply of raw materials, and "non-nucleus firms", most of which were closed, though very small firms whose premises and labour could not easily or usefully be employed for purposes of direct war work were allowed to carry on without nucleus status. Nucleus firms were required to provide for the care and maintenance of the plant and establishment of firms closed under a concentration scheme, and to take on the redundant elderly workers who were unsuitable for transfer to other industries; they were often obliged to take over the export orders of the closed firms, and the Government also encouraged them to supply goods at cost to closed firms to enable the latter to retain their identities and sales organisations.

Broadly speaking, the industries which have been concentrated are those which were growing rapidly before the war and which may be expected to expand again now that the war is over. The President of the Board of Trade, discussing their future, stated in July 1942 that the policy of concentration undoubtedly promoted industrial efficiency and that it would enable firms which had temporarily ceased production to restart after the war in more favourable conditions than if concentration had not been pursued. There had, he said, been the closest co-operation between the Board of Trade, the manufacturers and the Trade Unions concerned, and the policy had been applied in a flexible way, with no attempt to impose a rigid or uniform standard in different industries.

The results have been striking. Altogether, nearly 3,500 firms were closed under concentration schemes, and 65 million square feet of factory space released. In addition, over a quarter of a million workers, as a result of the contraction of industries in which concentration was applied, were made available for direct war-work.

With the progress of the war both concentration and the limitation of supplies by Government regulation were applied with increasing stringency. Some of the industries first brought within concentration schemes, such as jute, leather goods and toilet preparations, have, because of the increasing shortage of materials and the need to release still larger numbers of workers, been re-concentrated. At the same time, restrictions, not only on the quantity of a manufacturer's output but also on the kind of goods which may be produced, have been increased. The original Limitation of Supplies Orders, which dealt with groups of products, have been succeeded by a series of Control of Manufacture and Supply Orders, which cover most consumers' goods other than clothing and prohibit the manufacture of all but the most necessary articles : for example, in the glass-ware industry production is limited to the manufacture of tumblers, jugs, mugs and small mirrors ; of jewellery, only identification bracelets, cuff-links, studs and plain wedding-rings are allowed to be manufactured, and then only under licence. As a result, a very wide range of products has disappeared from the shops altogether, but a supply of the more essential goods has been maintained, though not without some difficulty.

Price Control

Prices of commodities other than food have been regulated by the Board of Trade since November 1939 under powers granted by the Prices of Goods Act and subsequently modified by later legislation. Both maximum retail prices and producers' profit margins are subject to regulations which are enforced by a Central Price Regulation Committee and local Committees, representative of manufacturers, traders and consumers in each of the Civil Defence regions. Any member of the public who suspects that he has been overcharged for an article may complain to his local committee, and if the latter conclude that a case has been made out, the facts are submitted to the central committee, which advises the Board of Trade as to whether a prosecution should be instituted. This method of control has ensured that falling supplies should not be accompanied by extravagant rises in prices of articles in common use, and though there have been some instances of rapid and unjustifiable increases in charges they have been relatively few. At the same time, the consumers' right to have complaints investigated has proved a valuable safeguard.

CHAPTER III

Restrictions on Consumption

RESTRICTIONS on the manufacture of consumers' goods had, inevitably, to be accompanied by some sort of restriction on consumption, and the experiences of the war of 1914–18 had shown how serious could be the results of an uncontrolled scramble for articles growing daily more scarce : necessities became luxuries, sometimes almost overnight ; prices rose with alarming swiftness, putting many articles of daily life out of the reach of those who needed them most, and profiteering added a new word—though not a new conception—to the vocabulary of the English language. In 1939 both the experts and the great mass of ordinary citizens were determined that these things should not happen again.

Nevertheless, the task of ensuring a fair distribution of supplies has not been easy. Much careful planning has been required to foresee, and obviate, future difficulties, and swift action has sometimes been called for to deal with problems arising from sudden and unexpected emergencies. On the whole, the success of the various measures of control adopted has been much greater than most people at the beginning of the war imagined to be possible : the general level of consumption has been progressively reduced and, though there have been some serious shortages and some real hardships, the general public has assented to stringent restrictions on their freedom of choice. They have done so willingly, because they realised the need for an ever-growing volume of war production and recognised that, with few and for the most part insignificant exceptions, these restrictions have in fact ensured the fairest possible distribution of the necessities and comforts of daily life.

The general problems involved have been approached from two distinct, though related, angles. On the one hand was the need to reduce the total volume of consumers' expenditure at a time when the growing volume of employment and a rising level of wages was producing a substantial increase in the total money income of the community, and on the other hand were the specific and detailed problems involved in cutting down the consumption of particular commodities.

The first of these problems has been tackled by increases in both direct and indirect taxation, designed not only to increase the National revenue but also to impose limits on the volume of private expenditure. The lower income groups have been brought within the field of income tax, and the standard rate of income tax now stands at 10s. in the £. At the same time, an ingenious system has provided that part of the extra tax (that resulting from certain reductions in the allowances and reliefs granted to income tax payers) shall be returned to them in the future as "post-war credits"—a method of compulsory saving that not only reduces current expenditure but which gives taxpayers a certain security for the future. Increases in taxation of all kinds have increased the proportion of the private income of the community as a whole taken up by the payment of taxes from 22 per cent. in 1938 and 25 per cent. in 1939 to 36 per cent. in 1944. While there has been an increase in the monetary volume of personal expenditure of 16 per cent. since 1938 (a figure which excludes indirect taxes payable on the various articles bought), personal expenditure measured in terms of constant prices was in 1944 only 80 per cent. of that in 1938.

The National Savings Movement

These changes in personal expenditure have been influenced by a series of campaigns conducted by the National Savings Movement, which have been planned to increase investment in National Savings Certificates and War Bonds. Press and poster advertising, schemes for the collection of small savings in factory, office and street savings groups have culminated each year in a special week of campaigning in every city, town and village in the country, with marches, processions and displays which both help to swell the total volume of savings and give a rare and welcome touch of pageantry to the drabness of everyday life in wartime. The National Savings

Movement has been criticised on the grounds that its propaganda is often guilty of muddled, and sometimes false, statements about the way in which savings contribute to the war effort, and also because, it is argued, the total volume of savings in any one week may be falsified by people withdrawing their savings within a short period of depositing them. While there is certainly substance in both these criticisms, there is no doubt that the National Savings Movement has played a valuable part in increasing the public awareness of the importance of savings to the war economy, and the Treasury's Analysis of the Sources of War Finance, presented with the 1944 Budget, shows that net personal savings had increased from £158,000,000 in the year 1938 to £1,407,000,000 in 1943.

Reduction in expenditure on specific types or classes of goods has, too, been brought about in a number of different ways. Propaganda of all kinds has been brought into use; some goods have disappeared from the shops altogether; and the distribution of many of the necessities of life has been organised through rationing.

Propaganda has been of particular importance in the field of public utility services where rationing would have been difficult or impossible. Posters urged the public to "Telephone Less" and "Telegraph Less", and still do so. Others stressed the importance of refraining from unnecessary travel, and while local authorities organised "Holidays at Home" festivities, such as dances, concerts, boxing displays, swimming galas and open-air theatres, a cartoon was exhibited by the Railway Companies showing the family who went away, only to find themselves caught in a railway-siding packed tightly with trucks full of munitions. The housewife was urged to "Travel between ten and four and leave rush-hour travel to war-workers, please". The employer is still advised to stagger working hours to reduce queueing during the rush periods, and the need for economy in the use of every kind of fuel is impressed upon everyone by means of posters, films and broadcasts.

Fuel Economy and Petrol Rationing

The fuel economy campaign is of particular interest, both because of the great, and still growing, difficulty in maintaining coal production at an adequate level and because this is the only field in which a rationing scheme was planned and then withdrawn as a result of criticism in Parliament and elsewhere. By 1942 the gap between consumption and output of coal in a full year was estimated to be in the region of 11 million tons, and hence, in order to conserve as much as possible of the total output for the use of war industries, it was proposed to ration domestic consumers, giving them a number of coupons, based on the size of the house, which could be expended either on gas, electricity, coke, coal or oil, or a combination of some or all of these. Criticism concentrated on the extreme administrative complexity of such a scheme, and its withdrawal was followed, in June 1942, by the opening of the first fuel economy campaign. Lighting in public buildings, shops and underground railways was reduced and restrictions, still in force, limited the use of central-heating and hot-water plants. Women's organisations, schools, clubs and other bodies were shown how comparatively small economies, such as the use of electric light bulbs of a lower wattage than usual, could mount to a really impressive total.

The response was good. By the end of the winter of 1942–43 it was announced that the amount of solid fuel delivered to domestic consumers was less than that which would have been required to meet the coupons under the rationing scheme. Nevertheless, at the end of 1943, the Minister of Fuel and Power, Major Lloyd George, warned domestic consumers that their consumption had again risen, and that the need for economy was greater than ever. During 1944 and the winter of 1944–45 coal deliveries to domestic consumers were limited to a few hundredweight a month, the precise amount varying in different areas.

The rationing of petrol for use in private cars was, in contrast, introduced at an early stage. At first, all motorists were allowed a small "basic ration". Later, however, allowances were granted only for business and other essential purposes, and then only if alternative means of transport were not available or if the applicant's age and physical condition made it necessary. Private cars almost disappeared from the roads. From June 1, 1945, however, a very small "basic" ration has again been allowed to every motorist.

Many other familiar features of pre-war life have disappeared too. Imported foods that were taken for granted in pre-war days, such as grapes, oranges and canned fruit and vegetables, have almost, and in some instances entirely, disappeared, along with many luxury products and manufactured foodstuffs. Paper rationing has severely restricted the output of both books and newspapers, with the result that books by popular authors are often out of print within a few days of publication, while magazines and newspapers can only be bought by those who have a regular order placed with their newsagent and by the lucky few who get to the news-stands at the moment when the wholesaler is making his deliveries. Clocks and watches are extremely scarce and no less extremely expensive, though imported alarm-clocks from the U.S.A. can be bought at controlled prices—for a considerable time these imported alarm-clocks were only available to those who could first satisfy the Board of Trade that their work was of sufficient importance, and their hour of rising sufficiently early, to justify the granting of a priority certificate. Cheap jewellery has disappeared from the fixed-price stores, along with steel saucepans, scourers, curtain rods and rings, and a host of other household goods. This list could, in fact, be extended for many pages, and further details will be found in chapters dealing with specific groups of commodities.

Rationing, which was first applied to the basic foodstuffs, has been extended to cover most items of ordinary diet, with the exception of bread and vegetables. Clothing, furniture and some other household goods have also been subject to rationing. The details of the different schemes, which are described in the chapters which follow, vary considerably, but all are designed with the same object: namely, to secure the fairest possible distribution of whatever supplies are available and to ensure, by the regulation of prices, that as far as possible the things that everybody needs shall be within the reach of all.

CHAPTER IV

The Distribution of Food

Rationing and Priority Allowances

THE MINISTRY OF FOOD'S organisation for the purchase of bulk supplies from abroad and the orderly distribution of both home-produced and imported foodstuffs from growers and manufacturers to the shops has been paralleled by an elaborate machinery set up to secure a fair distribution to consumers. Rationing, first of basic foodstuffs and later of a growing range of articles of daily diet, has been accompanied by the introduction of controlled schemes of distribution for a number of commodities for which rigid rationing was for one reason or another inappropriate, by the adoption of special measures for meeting the needs of "priority classes", by special arrangements for providing food for factory canteens and to agricultural workers, by the opening of "British Restaurants" and the control of food supplies to hotels and catering establishments of all kinds.

At the time of the Munich crisis in 1938, housewives were advised to keep a reserve of canned foods as an insurance against the risk of supplies being cut off on the outbreak of war. In the event, the outbreak of war made little, if any, difference to the housewife's ability to purchase in any quantity that she needed—or could afford—the various articles of diet to which her family was accustomed. The general public were, however, not surprised when, in January 1940, the first commodities—bacon, fats (butter, margarine and cooking fats) and sugar—were rationed. The rations were large—little, if at all, less than average peacetime consumption. In March 1940 meat rationing was introduced ; here, too, the ration was large and by fixing it by value instead of quantity the Ministry of Food gave the housewife a choice between buying a small amount of the more expensive cuts, or a larger amount of the cheaper cuts. Offals were, and have remained, unrationed, though a progressive reduction in the general meat ration has meant that liver, kidneys and tripe have joined the category of scarce luxuries. Tea was first rationed in July 1940, cheese in May 1941, and soap (rationed, too, by the Ministry of Food since the raw materials used also enter into food production) in February 1942.

For the purchase of all these basic commodities—with the exception of tea and soap, which may be bought anywhere—consumers are obliged to register with retailers. This regulation is designed to ensure that the flow of perishable commodities to the shops shall be enough—but not more than enough—to meet consumers' demands. Members of the Forces on leave and travellers, holiday-makers and others are, during an absence of a week or more from home, allowed to exchange their ration-book claim on their own retailer for a temporary ration card enabling them to buy food anywhere. With this exception, the consumer is allowed to change his retailer only when the annual issue of new ration books takes place or, at other times, with the special permission of a local Food Control Committee.

The permitted ration of basic foods has varied in accordance with the supply position. Where the ration of such an important protein food as cheese has had to be reduced, the cut has been counterbalanced by the issue of, for example, dried eggs or powdered milk. The weekly amount that may be spent on meat has varied between 2s. 2d. and 1s. 0d., most of the time being 1s. 2d. ; the amount of bacon which may be purchased has varied between 8 ounces and 3 ounces (generally 4 ounces), the amount of cheese between 8 ounces and one ounce, sugar between one pound and 8 ounces ;

the tea ration stood at 2 ounces until July 1945, when it was raised to 2½ ounces.

The general principle, in determining the size of basic rations, has been to provide the largest possible ration to all consumers rather than to provide larger rations for one specific class at the expense of another. There are, however, certain exceptions to this rule: first, special provisions are made for mothers and young children; secondly, a special ration of cheese is granted to men and women agricultural workers, underground miners and others who are prevented by the nature of their work from taking advantage of factory canteens; thirdly, special allowances are made to sick people whose illness makes a special diet necessary; and, fourthly, certain concessions in regard to the purchase of cheese, meat and fats are granted to vegetarians, Orthodox Jews and Moslems.

"Points" Rationing

An important addition to the general rationing scheme was made in 1941 by the adoption of a system of "grouped commodities" and of "points" rationing. At that time inequality of distribution of unrationed foods was producing many local shortages and, perhaps not less seriously, a sense of injustice among housewives who were apt, sometimes rightly, to attribute their inability to buy what they wanted not so much to the general scarcity as to the fact that others were getting more than their fair share. The "group" scheme enabled customers to buy each month, from a grocer with whom they were registered, a fixed quantity of either jam, marmalade, syrup or treacle. Later, mincemeat, fruit curd and imitation honey were added to the group, while syrup, treacle and imported canned marmalade were transferred to the points scheme. The total preserve ration has varied between 8 ounces and 2 pounds per month, and recently has been convertible into sugar, thus enabling housewives to buy sugar instead of jam. In addition, it has been usual to make a slight increase in the sugar ration for a few weeks during the summer so as to enable those who wish to do so to make jam. In fact, many families carefully hoard a part of their sugar ration throughout the year in order to increase the quantity of preserves that can be made at home.

The "points" scheme, which was originally confined to canned fish, canned meat and canned beans, entitles each holder of a ration book to purchase to the value of a certain number of points per month. Points values are then attached to each of the commodities falling within the scheme, and the consumer has a free choice within the limits set by the total number of points to which he—or she—is entitled. The fairness of this method of distribution has done much to add to the public's appreciation of the work of the Ministry of Food, and the scheme has been extended to cover a very wide variety of products, including canned fruits, canned peas, tomatoes and milk, rice, sago, tapioca, dried pulses, cereal breakfast foods and oatflakes, biscuits, and dried fruits of all kinds. No registration with retailers is required and purchases may be made from any shop with the necessary stocks. Points values are varied from time to time to meet changes in the supply position and in public demand. Thus, the number of points needed to purchase a tin of salmon—a normal and very popular article of diet in British working-class households in peacetime—has been increased since points-rationing was first introduced, while the number of points needed to buy tinned pilchards—an equally nutritious but much less sought after food—has been reduced.

The distribution of some other important foods, though not strictly rationed, is subject to a measure of control designed to ensure that everyone gets a fair share and that priority allowances are available for those who need them. For some foods, such as milk, customers are obliged to register with retailers ; for others, of which oranges are an example, no registration is required, but purchases must be recorded in the customer's ration book. Young children and expectant mothers are given the first claim on supplies of milk, fresh and dried eggs, and oranges. Special ration books are issued for children and an expectant mother is entitled to receive, and to use, a child's ration book in addition to her own, and the importance of doing so is stressed at maternity and child welfare centres. The priority allowance of fresh eggs to children between six and eighteen months old is usually at the rate of three per week ; the allowance of milk varies according to the age of the child from three and a half to fourteen pints per week : the allotted amounts are guaranteed throughout the year, irrespective of the general supply position, while, on the other hand, the allowance of milk to ordinary consumers varies seasonally from two pints per week to four. Retailers are supplied with enough milk to meet all their priority and non-priority claims together with a small margin for emergencies. The small milk ration has been a sad privation and a considerable source of discontent to non-priority consumers. But, on the other hand, most people realise that by basing distribution on the needs rather than the means of consumers a valuable social reform has been achieved and that the result should be an incalculable benefit to the health of the new generation.

Priority allowances under the National Milk Scheme are provided at a reduced price or free of cost; and coupled with this is the National Vitamins Scheme, which guarantees, again either free or at low cost, a supply of essential vitamins to those who need them most. Children of school age are provided with milk and meals in school, and to-day a large percentage of the school population receives milk in school every day, while an increasing proportion take their midday meal at school, receiving both either free or for a small payment.

Canteens

Results show the measures described above to have proved themselves an outstanding success. Wartime figures of maternal mortality and infant death rates were the lowest on record, and doctors agree that the health of the child population, taking the country as a whole, has improved since 1939. For adults, the standard ration is sufficient, but not more than sufficient, to maintain health. But here, too, extra provisions have been made. Factories employing more than 250 workers have been required to provide facilities for hot meals, and since 1940 the number of factory canteens has been enormously increased and workers are officially encouraged to "spread the ration" by taking meals at work. (No coupons are surrendered for meals taken away from home, whether in canteens or restaurants.) Food is allocated to canteens and other catering establishments on the basis of the number of meals served, and larger allowances are given to the canteens of factories where the work is of an especially heavy character.

British Restaurants

For office workers and others for whom canteens are not available there are British Restaurants, run either by local authorities, voluntary organisations, or as a part of the school meals service. Originally set up in London in the autumn of 1940 to provide hot meals for those who were homeless or without fuel as a result of the "blitz", they have now become a national institution, providing wholesome, well-balanced meals at low prices, and open to anyone who cares to use them. In London alone 250 restaurants are provided by the Londoners' Meals Service of the London County Council, as well as a number organised by voluntary societies. Almost every town with a population of 50,000 or more (as well as many smaller local government areas) has at least one British Restaurant, and the total throughout the country is now in excess of 2,000, serving an average of about 600,000 meals per day. Though locally administered, the capital cost of these restaurants is borne by the Ministry of Food, and the Ministry supplies such items of equipment as stoves, crockery and kitchen utensils which it would otherwise be difficult or impossible to obtain. Existing buildings are used wherever possible, and power to requisition suitable premises has been delegated to local authorities which, with the assistance of the Ministry, have succeeded in adapting large private houses, halls, schools and even churches to this new use. Prices are fixed to cover running expenses and to yield a surplus of one per cent. per annum for the amortization of capital costs. Typical charges are 2d. for a plate of soup, 8d. for a main dish of meat and two vegetables, 2d. or 3d. for a sweet, and 1d. or 1½d. for a cup of tea. The quantities of rationed foods which may be sold for use in British Restaurants are based, like the allowances to commercial establishments, on the number of meals served, but where at least 60 per cent. of the regular customers are industrial workers the scale of allowable purchases is increased to the level permitted to industrial canteens.

The Ministry of Food has, from the start, concerned itself with the nutritional standard of the meals served in British Restaurants. General advice, and the issue of an expertly written booklet on canteen catering, have been followed by a planned survey of the dietetic value of meals served in industrial canteens and British Restaurants, and useful conclusions have been reached. It is hoped that eventually clinical workers will be able to examine the health of people taking the meals and correlate their observations with the findings of the nutritional advisers; already much valuable information has been gained which can be used to assess the part that communal feeding can play in raising the standard of the nation's health.

Looking back, it is astonishing to realise that a service which was hastily improvised to meet a desperate, though temporary, need, should have developed in such a rapid and orderly way and should have met with such wide and general praise. The general standard of meals is high, and, indeed, the chief criticism has come not from consumers but from commercial caterers who regard these establishments as an actual or potential threat to their own businesses. However, as long ago as January 1942 Lord Woolton, who was then Minister of Food, gave an assurance to the catering trade that a local inspection would be made by the Ministry in any area in which it was proposed to open a British Restaurant and where the local caterers considered it unnecessary, and that permission to proceed with plans would depend on the findings of such inquiries.

MAKE-DO AND MEND—*Above, child's siren-suit made by her mother from an old coat. Below, utility furniture and china.*

UTILITY CLOTHES, *designed to save labour and materials, were smart and inexpensive.*

(By courtesy of "Vogue")

BRITISH RESTAURANT *The Fishmongers Company lent their famous banqueting-hall to the London County Council for use as a restaurant. As many as a thousand lunches were served daily.*

FOOD CONTROL—*Above, one week's rations for an adult. Below, orange juice was available for every child under five.*

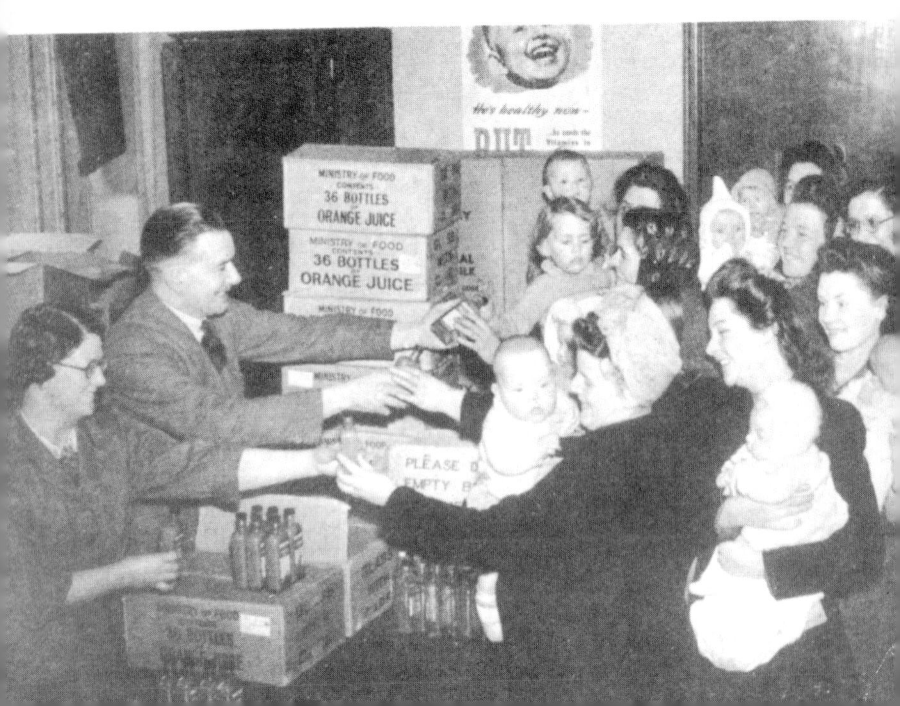

Emergency Meals

In addition, a network of Emergency Meals Centres was organised throughout the country to cater after air raids both for the homeless and for those who, because of the interruption of public services, were unable to cook in their own homes. In London the provisions made were sufficient to provide meals for 25 per cent. of the population at any one time, while for less vulnerable areas provision was made for from 10 to 20 per cent. The centres were dispersed in different parts of the towns that they were intended to serve, and were equipped with stoves burning solid fuel, which made them independent of gas and electricity services. Each was supplied with a reserve of food and most of them had also a reserve of water as a safeguard against the interruption of public water supplies. Cooking depots were also established outside, but within reach of, target areas, from which freshly cooked food could be distributed in insulated containers to points within a radius of about 15 miles. Like British Restaurants, these depots were improvised to meet blitz conditions, and the first was opened at Sheffield after a heavy raid on that city in the winter of 1940–41 ; they were maintained in full working order to meet any sudden emergency, and the staff employed were used to cook meals which were dispatched daily to large numbers of schools, British Restaurants and works canteens.

A third type of provision for emergencies was that organised to provide meals and hot drinks in air-raid shelters. Responsibility for shelter feeding was undertaken by local authorities, and detailed arrangements were made, under their supervision, by caterers or voluntary bodies, while in London the London Passenger Transport Board operated a canteen service, as the agent of the Ministry of Food, to supply the needs of the large numbers of people who took shelter in Underground stations during air raids. In London more than 2,500 air-raid shelters, with accommodation for nearly 900,000 people, had canteen facilities, and in the provinces shelter-canteens were provided in 145 of the more vulnerable local government areas.

The Control of Food Prices

Another and most important aspect of food policy has been the control of prices : a control designed both to prevent inflation through the stabilisation of the cost of living and to ensure fair distribution of supplies. The prices of many essential foods were controlled immediately on the outbreak of war, and stand-still orders were introduced to enable the Ministry of Food to investigate costs and determine the levels at which prices should be fixed. Inevitably, however, a rise in costs due to circumstances arising from the war began to make itself felt, and by the end of 1939 the Ministry of Labour's cost-of-living index showed a rise of about 12 per cent. Food and house rent are the most important elements in this index: the latter had already been stabilised by the Rent Restriction Acts, and in January 1940 the Chancellor of the Exchequer announced to the House of Commons that the Government had begun to peg food prices by the introduction of subsidies. In April 1941 the Government announced their decision to continue and extend the policy of stabilisation in order to maintain the cost-of-living index at an average level of not more than 25–30 per cent. above that of the immediate pre-war period. This policy was successfully maintained, though at the cost of large Government subsidies, until 1944, when Sir John Anderson, then Chancellor of the Exchequer, announced in his budget speech a modification designed to allow rising costs to be reflected by a small—and still much less than proportionate—rise in prices.

When the policy of price stabilisation was first introduced subsidies were already being paid at the rate of about £50,000,000 a year. By 1943 this figure had increased to £150,000,000, of which £35,000,000 a year was being used to keep down the price of bread, £23,000,000 to subsidise meat, and a similar amount to subsidise potatoes, while sums varying between £10–£20,000,000 were being expended on stabilising the prices of milk, eggs and sugar, and smaller amounts on tea, bacon, milk products and other items. Measured in terms of retail prices, these subsidies represent a reduction in the price of bread of 2d. per quartern, of potatoes by 3½d. per 7 pounds, of meat by 1½d. per pound, and of sugar by a fraction less than 2½d. per pound. In addition, price control has also been applied to a constantly widening range of food products which receive no subsidy or which are subsidised only in respect of some of their ingredients. At the end of March 1945 subsidies were running at the rate of £225,000,000.

It has not been easy to devise methods of price control which are fair, reasonably simple in application and easy to operate, but the Ministry of Food, which is responsible for the control of all food prices, has shown quite remarkable skill and ingenuity in adapting the general policy to meet the particular circumstances of the different branches of the food trades. Mistakes have been few, and have been quickly remedied: indeed, the whole job has been carried out not only with thoroughness, which might have been expected, but with a degree of elasticity which in pre-war days was not generally considered to be within the power of a Government

Department. Thus, for example, the schedule of maximum prices for meat, which is inevitably long owing to the different methods of cutting used by butchers in various parts of the country, was in December 1942 simplified to an extent which reduced the total number of beef items specified from sixty to ten—a reform which eased the work of both buyers and sellers of meat and of the officials concerned with enforcement of regulations. Again, a change of another kind was made when, in the autumn of 1942, the shipping position made it necessary to cut down the consumption of bread: to keep bread off the list of rationed foods was then, and has continued to be, a permanent part of Government policy; hence it was decided to raise the price of bread while at the same time reducing the price of potatoes, in the hope that consumers would increase their purchases of the latter at the expense of the former. The reason for the change was explained to the public through advertisements and broadcast talks; people were told how and why to economise in the use of bread and publicity was given to new ways of cooking potatoes. This combination of price changes with a propaganda drive has since been applied in other instances where it has been considered desirable to increase or decrease the consumption of certain foods.

Problems of Price and Distribution

One of the main difficulties which have arisen from the control of prices is that the excess of demand over supply tends to result in stocks being disposed of in the areas in which they are produced, since transport to more distant localities involves costs which the producer need not incur if he disposes of his stocks locally. Here, too, the methods used to secure " fair shares " for everybody have varied. With certain fruits and vegetables maximum prices are fixed by areas in a way designed to attract sellers to send their products to areas of relative scarcity; with some other unrationed foodstuffs the Ministry of Food itself undertakes distribution from the point of manufacture or importation to localities where stocks are released to traders; with others again—of which potatoes are probably the most important instance—the Ministry purchases stocks in the areas in which there is a surplus and sells them to traders in areas where supplies are inadequate; and finally, with many manufactured food products wholesalers are requested to allocate to their retail customers quantities proportionate to those sold before the war, but modified in accordance with wartime changes in the distribution of population.

Not all these methods have been equally successful. For example with poultry and rabbits the introduction of a price differential in favour of sellers in urban areas has not completely overcome the tendency for supplies to be consumed mainly in the areas in which they are produced, and the same problem, though in a less severe form, is still being encountered in the distribution of soft fruits such as strawberries and raspberries. On the other hand, a widespread public demand during the early summer of 1944 for the price of lettuces to be brought under control indicates that, in spite of many difficulties, the application of price control to green vegetables which was first introduced in 1943, has proved of real value to domestic consumers. Control of fish prices, though complicated, has also operated to the advantage of consumers, and the same can be said of the methods adopted to control prices of manufactured foodstuffs, many of which are grouped according to quality with a maximum price common to the products of all manufacturers within a particular range. A curious instance is that of eggs, where the price paid to the producer is higher than that charged to the consumer: this apparently inexplicable arrangement was deliberately, and indeed cleverly, devised to enable the Ministry to direct the supply of all home-produced eggs from producers to consumers All poultry keepers, with the exception of those possessing not more than twenty-five birds, are required to sell only to a licensed buyer or packing station, from whom they receive the price fixed by the Ministry. From that stage onwards the eggs are distributed under Ministry instructions and a subsidy is used to bridge the gap between the selling price and the buying price.

The list of commodities whose prices are controlled by the Ministry of Food now includes most everyday articles of diet as well as a large number of foods which, as a result of the war, have become difficult to obtain. Usually control is applied at all stages through which an article passes on its way from the grower, importer or manufacturer to the ultimate consumer, so that both producers and wholesalers, as well as retailers, can sell only at, or below, the maximum fixed by the Ministry. Prices of the few types of food not subject to price control—such as hot-house grapes, peaches, melons and mushrooms—are often fantastically high, and the ordinary consumer, as he gazes through a shop window and wonders who is to buy these fabulous luxuries, measures the rise in their prices against the much smaller rise in the price of controlled foods and realises dimly the important part that price control has played in wartime domestic economy.

After its initial successes in controlling the price of foodstuffs, i was inevitable that the Ministry of Food should have been asked to control the prices of meals in restaurants—mainly with the object of preventing the more expensive restaurants from obtaining an excessively large share of scarce foods, and of diminishing the amount of " luxury eating ". No restaurant is allowed to serve a meal of more than three courses, only one of which may contain meat or fish, and the maximum charge for a meal, exclusive of beverages, is fixed at 5s., though restaurants and hotels with exceptionally heavy overhead charges or which provide facilities for dancing or cabaret shows are allowed to make additional charges in respect of these ; such additional charges can only be made after official sanction has been obtained, and in fact only a small number of restaurants in London and the larger provincial towns are permitted to exceed the 5s. maximum. The general effect of this regulation has been to reduce the price (as well, of course, as the quantity and quality) of meals in the more expensive restaurants, while in many of the cheaper restaurants rising costs have been followed by increased charges. At the same time, the general adoption of " austerity " meals, though producing only a relatively small saving in food consumption, has tended to even out the distribution of supplies of such things as poultry, game and the more expensive types of fish, and was welcomed for its importance as a gesture at a time when people as a whole were anxious to make equality of sacrifice something more than an empty and meaningless phrase.

The Relation between Central and Local Control

Enforcement of the complicated series of regulations described in the preceding paragraphs has proved less difficult than might have been anticipated, and for two reasons. First, the policy, adopted by the Ministry of Food from the outset, of using ordinary trade channels of distribution and of bringing into the Ministry experts with an intimate knowledge of the trades whose problems were to be their concern, made it possible to adapt existing trade practices to wartime uses and to carry out any change of policy with the utmost speed and smoothness ; and, secondly, the use of local Food Control Committees in each area for dealing with rationing and the licensing of shops has made it possible to combine the maximum use of local knowledge and experience with the minimum of interference with custom and tradition.

The general direction of policy is, of course, the responsibility of the Minister, and all the broader decisions, as well as many points of detail, have to be made at headquarters. On the other hand, much of the day-to-day administration is devolved upon the nineteen Divisional Food Officers, each of whom is in charge of one of the regions into which the United Kingdom is divided for administrative purposes. The duties of the Divisional Food Officers have included the maintenance of reserve supplies of food in each area as a contingency against air raids or the risk of invasion ; the supervision of all emergency feeding arrangements ; the supply and distribution of food for everyday consumption ; the supervision of local food offices ; the correct interpretation of the regulations governing rationing ; the enforcement of regulations ; the provision of transport and warehouse accommodation, as well as the making of statistical returns and the performance of the normal establishment duties connected with a Government department. Each divisional organisation was planned to enable it to become entirely independent of the Ministry's headquarters, should such independence ever have become necessary.

Each division is further subdivided into local food control areas, and the local authorities are responsible, subject to the approval of the Ministry, for the appointment of the Food Control Committee in their district. There are now about 1,500 Food Control Committees in operation, each consisting of fifteen members, five of whom are appointed to represent the various branches of the retail food trade, including the Co-operative movement, and the remainder (of whom at least two must be women) to represent the interests of consumers. Food Control Committees are responsible for the enforcement of the Ministry's regulations within the locality which they cover, and have power to prosecute offenders ; they deal with the issue of licences to traders, though the final decision as to whether a licence shall be granted rests with the Ministry ; and they can grant or withhold permission to members of the public who wish to change their registrations with retailers during the currency of their ration books. The usefulness of these committees, however, is not limited to the functions thus briefly listed. The representative character of the average membership means that many minor grievances and injustices can be dealt with quickly and informally before they reach serious proportions.

Nutrition and Food Education

Planning of food policy is greatly assisted by the existence within the Ministry of Food of an expert scientific staff, headed by Professor J. C. Drummond, who is known throughout the world for his work on nutrition. In the Ministry's experimental kitchens, experiments are made in the use of new food products and in methods of obtaining the maximum nutritional value from familiar foodstuffs. In addition, Bulletins are sent regularly to teachers of domestic science for use in schools, to women's organisations such as the Women's Voluntary Services and the Women's Institutes, and to the gas and electricity companies. Dieticians give talks on nutritional problems to mothers at ante-natal clinics and infant welfare centres and provide refresher courses for cookery demonstrators and rural teachers of domestic economy.

Food advice organisers are attached to each divisional food office, and are responsible for organising centres at which housewives can see demonstrations of new ways of preparing food and can ask questions about their particular problems. These centres now exist in the main streets of many towns ; they are educational, and not propagandist, in character : their purpose is not to tell the housewife how well off she is in comparison with women in Continental Europe, but to show her how to make the best and most intelligent use of the food at her disposal. From these centres demonstrators go to give advice in canteens, at meetings of women's organisations and in the out-patients' department of hospitals. Broadcast talks, films, and advertisements in newspapers and women's magazines give the latest news from the " Kitchen Front "—information which varies from instructions on how to apply for a new ration book to recipes for making dried-egg omelettes or the national dishes of other countries. This constant stream of advice and information has done much to maintain the nation's health by stressing the importance of salads and fresh vegetables, and by teaching the average housewife to give her family a properly balanced diet ; it has done at least as much, and possibly even more, in showing her how to make the most familiar ingredients into dishes that are not merely edible but even delicious : thus, for example, a persistent campaign on the correct method of cooking cabbage is beginning at last to do away with one of the traditional horrors of the English kitchen, while at the same time the revival of forgotten recipes by celebrated cooks of the past is showing women that limited ingredients can still be used to produce meals of an almost infinite variety.

CHAPTER V

Clothes

IN THE PERIOD between the two wars the standard of dress in Britain, both for men and women, rose steadily and fast. An increasing variety in materials was accompanied by a general improvement in design and cut, and by a substantial reduction in prices. Mass-production methods had largely, though not altogether, ousted the little dressmaker and the small tailor, cutting and making up suits in his own workroom. Made-to-measure clothes were, for the most part, a luxury for the well-to-do, but for those who bought off the peg the range of choice, in style, quality and price, was so wide that for the average adult—and particularly the average woman—the problem had ceased to be simply that of finding a garment to fit and had become the more complex but also more amusing one of deciding what she really wanted, and then of making up her mind whether she could afford it.

With war, the problem changed again, and the fact that millions of the adult population were in uniform did not—for obvious reasons—ease the difficulties of the millions who were not. The need to release labour and conserve materials resulted in an unparalleled restriction on the consumer's freedom of choice ; and yet, as observers from other countries have frequently pointed out, most women appear to be better dressed, and are certainly dressed in better taste, than they were five years ago. What this improvement has cost in terms of individual thought and effort it is impossible to estimate. Wartime restrictions have taught many women to substitute ingenuity for extravagance. But they have done more than that. The Board of Trade, which has been responsible for securing an orderly reduction in civilian consumption, has also played an important part in raising the general level of public taste and in teaching people how to make the most of the limited supplies available to them.

Restrictions have operated in three ways : first, through the organised limitation of supplies, described in a previous chapter ; secondly, through the rationing of civilian clothing ; and thirdly,

POSTERS *discouraged people from unnecessary telegraphing, telephoning and travel.*

through the introduction of "austerity" fashions and the production of a large percentage of clothing to "utility" specifications. Parallel with these limitations on the consumer's freedom of choice has been the development of a price-fixing machinery designed to safeguard the purchaser and to prevent profiteering, and the use of both advertising and educational channels to help women to buy wisely and to keep their own and their families' clothes in good repair. These measures are described in detail in the pages which follow.

Rationing of Clothes

Although restrictions on production were introduced soon after the outbreak of war, the consumer's freedom to buy was limited, until June 1941, only by what he could find in the shops. The first effect of the Limitation of Supplies Orders was to reduce stocks rather than to limit the quantities available to the domestic purchaser, and for many months after the outbreak of war retail sales continued, in spite of rising prices, to increase. By the beginning of 1941 a shortage of some types of clothing was becoming noticeable, but there was no general shortage, and it was perhaps for this reason that the introduction, in June 1941, of clothes rationing came to most people as a complete surprise. The need for rationing, once explained, was generally understood, and most people accepted the new restrictions willingly and cheerfully as they counted their coupons and estimated how far they could be made to go.

For many people the restrictions were, even at the start, severe. Every article of clothing, with the exception of hats and industrial overalls (the latter were brought into the scheme later), was rationed, and its coupon value announced. Each civilian, man, woman and child, was given an allowance of 66 coupons for the first year of rationing, and it was expected that these would be sufficient to enable everyone to maintain an adequate, but not more than adequate, wardrobe. The amount of clothing which could be purchased with 66 coupons was estimated to be just about half the quantity bought by the average civilian in a year in normal times. A man's ration was enough to enable him to buy little more than he stood up in : a suit required 26 coupons, a shirt 5, a tie one, woollen vest and trunks 8, socks 3 and shoes 7, leaving him 16 coupons with which he could buy handkerchiefs at one per coupon, pyjamas at

COMMON SENSE *about cooking and eating was illustrated in Ministry of Food posters.*

8 coupons a suit, or a dressing-gown for 8 coupons. A woman needed 18 coupons for a suit or overcoat, 11 for a woollen dress with sleeves or 7 for a dress of material other than wool, 5 for shoes and 2 for stockings, one each for brassiere and suspender belt and 3 each for vest and knickers. Clothing in sizes suitable for children under four years of age was coupon-free, and clothing for other children was rated at a lower coupon-value than similar articles for adult use, thus making available for them larger quantities than their parents were permitted to purchase for their own use. No coupons were generally required for second-hand clothing, but maximum prices were fixed, above which purchases could not be made without the surrender of coupons, thus ensuring that articles "as good as new" could only be bought instead of, and not in addition to, new clothes.

There was, inevitably, a considerable amount of criticism of detail, and the scheme has since been modified, partly to meet some of these criticisms and partly because of the need to cut down consumption still further. At the end of the first ration year the ration was cut by about 22 per cent. by reducing the total number of coupons, extending the period over which they were to be used, and by changing the coupon-value of certain articles. This last method has been used to assist the sale of stocks which might otherwise become useless or to restrict the demand for articles that are abnormally scarce : thus in the summer of 1941 reductions were made in the coupon-value of certain types of summer clothing to enable stocks to be cleared, and articles damaged in air raids could be sold at reduced coupon-value, provided the prices did not exceed a certain prescribed maximum. On the other hand, women's leather-soled shoes now require 7 coupons, while shoes with wooden soles need only 2 ; again, the shortage of fully-fashioned stockings has led to their being up-pointed from 2 coupons to 3 and seamless rayon stockings being down-pointed from 2 to 1½. The ingenuity of women who evaded the regulations by making dresses and other personal clothing from furnishing fabrics was countered by the extension of the rationing scheme to these materials, and to-day the manufacture of furnishing fabrics is largely prohibited, while coupons have to be given up for curtains (other than those made from net), loose covers and towels. During the war black-out material was coupon-free, but in September 1945 it was put on coupons.

Criticisms of the Scheme

Criticism has centred around three main problems. First, while the scheme has undoubtedly secured a certain rough justice in distribution, those with large stocks of good quality clothes have inevitably been at an advantage compared with those whose stocks, when rationing started, were low or of poor quality, and with the passage of time the difficulties of those with few reserves to fall back on have necessarily increased, as is suggested by the fact that each release of coupons for use is followed by a rush of buying which diminishes until the end of the coupon period, when sales fall to a very low level. It has sometimes been suggested that it might have been possible to secure a more equitable distribution by placing a higher coupon-value on better quality articles, as has in fact been done with women's shoes and stockings, but the administrative difficulties would have been considerable and, in view of the fact that most clothing is now made to conform to utility specifications, the result would have been small. It is certain, however, that the war has taught many people something of their grandparents' appreciation of the value of durability, though how much of this appreciation will survive when plenty returns it is difficult to guess.

Other criticisms have been directed to the supply of children's clothing and of overalls to industrial workers. Babies' made-up clothing was brought within the rationing scheme in August 1941, and ration cards for babies were issued, while expectant mothers were given a special ration of 50 coupons, later increased to 60, to cover their special needs and to buy articles required for the layette. Special allowances for older children and for those growing abnormally quickly were also introduced and have been modified from time to time. Many mothers feel that these allowances are insufficient. Older children have, in fact, had more coupons spent on them than has any other section of the community. On the other hand, in some instances the coupons of younger children have been used to buy articles for adult use. In any case, since a larger ration could only be made available by cutting down still further the quantities available for adults or by the diversion of labour and materials required for direct war production, every effort has to be made to ensure that the utmost possible wear is obtained for every coupon spent. Thus, though knitting-wool is rationed, the Board of Trade points out that fewer coupons are required to buy the wool to make a sweater or a pair of socks than would be needed if the article itself were purchased; Make-do and Mend classes (referred to elsewhere) help the housewife to cut down outworn adult garments and remake them for children. Many schools have schemes to assist in the passing on of outworn clothes to smaller children, and, on behalf of the Board of Trade, the Women's Voluntary Services have organised more than 500

Clothing and Shoe Exchanges all over the country for the same purpose.

Industrial Clothing

It has already been stated that when rationing was first introduced certain types of industrial overalls could be bought without coupons. The result, not surprisingly, was that these garments were widely purchased for ordinary domestic use, to save wear on precious " good clothes ". The concession had therefore to be cancelled, and arrangements were made instead to distribute overalls to industrial workers at reduced coupon-rates. Coupons must be given up whether the worker buys the overalls himself or receives them from his employer. Where a firm takes on new workers who have not enough coupons to " pay " for their overalls, the Board of Trade makes a loan of coupons to enable the firm to get the overalls it needs, and the loan is then repaid by the collection of coupons from the workers in instalments over a period.

Apart from this scheme for providing industrial overalls, the Board of Trade issues 10 extra coupons to nearly all industrial and agricultural workers. This arrangement was made after consultation with employers and Trades Unions as to the needs of workers in different industries, and was designed to help these workers to replace clothes which had been subjected to exceptional wear and tear. Workers in the heaviest industries can also apply for extra coupons from a small hardship pool administered by a joint committee at the various works.

A survey of coupon expenditure showed at the end of the first year an average of 3 coupons in hand per person; but many people had obviously run right out. Expenditure by women was slightly higher than that by men, but inquiry showed little justification for the fear that husbands would be stripped of their coupons by their wives. During the first year men spent 26 per cent. of their coupons on shirts and underwear, 17 per cent. on boots and shoes, 15 per cent. on socks and 22 per cent. on suits, jackets and trousers. The remaining 20 per cent. had to cover all other requirements. During the second year these proportions remained substantially unchanged, apart from a fall in the percentage spent on suits, jackets and trousers. Women spent during the first year 18 per cent. on underwear and 23 per cent. on frocks and coats, jackets and skirts. During the second year there was a slight reduction in the purchases of underwear and a corresponding increase in expenditure on outer garments.

The savings effected by rationing have been very large indeed. At the end of the first year it was estimated that 250,000 tons of shipping space had been freed for the carriage of essential war materials, and 400,000 men and women released for the Forces or war industry; reduction in consumers' expenditure amounted to £300,000,000, a figure all the more impressive in view of the rise in personal incomes during the period.

"Utility" and "Austerity"

Effective as clothes rationing has been in restricting consumption, it did not and could not by itself ensure that the right types of goods were produced or that they were produced at the right prices. Clothes prices, which had risen in April 1941 to 72 per cent. above the 1939 level, rose another 23 per cent. in the following year. At the same time, manufacturers, restricted by Limitation of Supplies Orders as to their total output, tended to concentrate on the production of higher priced goods, with the result that, in spite of rationing, many of the cheaper grades of clothing became practically unobtainable.

It was primarily to meet these difficulties that the Utility Scheme was introduced by the Board of Trade in 1941. The scheme was devised to ensure that a proportion of all the essential articles of clothing manufactured should be made to simple specifications which, while ensuring the greatest possible economy in materials and labour, would at the same time keep costs as low as possible and, by the standardisation of the finished articles, make possible a satisfactory system of price control. The task, thus defined, proved by no means easy to carry out. The first stage was to draw up a roughly defined series of categories, with maximum prices for articles falling within each category, but without any precise definition of quality. Some of the early utility products were in fact of excellent quality, but others were so poor as to jeopardise, for their purchasers, the reputation of the now famous utility mark: CC41. However, the system of control was rapidly extended; with the help of the various trade associations concerned, precise specifications were drawn up, and within a few months the public had become familiar with a wide range both of utility clothes and utility fabrics.

To-day about 80 per cent. of all clothing and materials sold by the yard for civilian use in this country conform to utility specifications, and utility production has been extended to many other types of goods, of which details are given elsewhere in this booklet. Utility production, though standardised within certain limits, does not mean that manufacturers are obliged to conform to a single pattern for each type of garment. In fact, the customer still has a wide range of choice in most kinds of materials and finished garments, but sizes and the quantity and quality of materials used are regulated, and manufacturers are prohibited from making up utility fabrics into other than utility garments. The description of an article as "utility" and the use of the utility mark already referred to is permitted only when the Board of Trade is satisfied that the producer has conformed with all the regulations laid down, and the mark is thus a guarantee to the consumer of a certain standard of quality.

The administrative difficulties involved in securing any substantial measure of standardisation in a branch of industry as diverse as are most sections of the clothing trades have been considerable. Co-operation between the Board of Trade and representatives of the industries concerned has by this time produced a successful solution of many, though by no means all, of the problems involved. Some utility production has been of a lower quality than consumers felt they had a right to expect. The quality of shoes, especially children's shoes, rayon stockings and corsets has been very widely criticised, and official explanations to the effect that raw material supplies make the production of better quality goods possible only at the expense of some more vital branch of the war effort have not always been well received by women, who feel that they are spending far too many of their precious coupons on these all too perishable necessities. On the other hand, the quality, style and price of most utility garments have made them widely popular, even among many women who before the war usually bought more than averagely expensive clothes.

Simplicity and Smartness

The disappearance of almost all fussiness in clothes can be traced to two causes, apart from the personal predilections of their designers. The first was the need to keep down prices, and the second (which represents only another way of looking at the same problem) was the need to economise in labour and materials. Price control was, and remains, an essential part of the Utility Scheme. Control is exercised at every stage of production and distribution, down to the retail sale to the ultimate consumer, and this control, coupled with the absence of purchase tax on utility clothing, has resulted in a substantial reduction in prices.

Economy in labour and materials has been secured by an elaborate series of regulations which limit the freedom of the designers and manufacturers of both utility and non-utility clothes. These "austerity" provisions forbid the use of embroidery, and of appliqué work and lace on lingerie; they place limits on the depth of hems and on the number of seams allowed in garments of different kinds; they restrict the use of tucks, pleats and buttons, and prohibit the use of velvet, fur, fur fabric and several other materials for the trimming of women's coats and jackets. The original "austerity" regulations controlling the production of men's clothing forbade, among other things, the making of double-breasted jackets and of trousers with permanent turn-ups; they limited the amount of stitching permitted in a suit, the number of buttons that might be used and—in the face of wide popular protests—the number of pockets in a man's jacket to three, in waistcoats to two, and in trousers to three.

Some of these regulations are tiresome and a few are foolish. Taken together they tend, inevitably, to make for monotony in dress. But, as far as women's clothes are concerned, the combined effect of high-quality design for utility clothes and an enforced austerity in clothes of all kinds has been astonishingly good. The average woman's clothes may not be of as good material as they were in pre-war days, and, as has already been stated, her shoes and stockings are certainly very much inferior, but the total impression which she makes is neater, often smarter, usually altogether more chic. Forced to do without frills, she has learned something of the French woman's appreciation of cut and line; limited by rationing to something less than half of her pre-war purchases, she has learned that colour, to be used with effect, must also be used with discretion and that the casual buying of clothes that happen to catch the eye is anything but a safeguard against the risk of having "nothing to wear". Most judges agree that this improvement in public taste has come to stay, and that when the relaxation of wartime restrictions gives women a wider freedom of choice in design and materials, the lessons learned during the past three or four years will not be forgotten: indeed, the traditionally high quality of British materials, when combined with present standards of taste, should greatly enhance London's importance as a centre of fashion not only for tailored clothes but for every variety of women's dress.

As far as men are concerned, the effect of austerity regulations was, from the first, much less happy. Restrictions on the length of shirts and socks were accepted, not without protest, and the quantity of material saved by these modifications was substantial. But male conservatism reacted violently against the prohibition of trouser turn-ups and other limitations on freedom of choice in the style of outer garments. At last, in January 1944, the President of the Board of Trade announced that since plans were being made to provide suits of normal peacetime design to men demobilised from the Forces, it would be impracticable to retain restrictions on suits designed for the general public. It was therefore decided that restrictions on the design of men's suits should be lifted, while the coupon-value of " austerity " suits should be reduced so as to clear stocks.

This episode, which represents perhaps the only major failure in the Board of Trade's austerity policy, is of some importance as an example—of which many more could be quoted—of the way in which Government policy has shown itself responsive to the wishes as well as the needs of consumers. It is remarkable, too, that in the vast complex of regulations so few mistakes should have been made in securing the necessary economies.

Consumer Surveys

An important reason for the success of the measures described in the preceding paragraphs has been the close relationship established between the Board of Trade and representative sections of producers, retailers and consumers. While representatives of manufacturers and traders advise the Department on technical problems, a Consumer Panel of 10,000 men and women has provided sample information on which it has been possible to make estimates of the total necessary annual production of different types of garments. A periodic check of the entire wardrobes of members of the panel has made it possible to assess the effect of rationing on different classes and to check trade claims as to the demand for particular articles. Three thousand members of the general public are also questioned monthly as to their difficulties in purchasing essential items, and the information thus gathered is supplemented by visits to shops to check current shortages. In addition, special surveys by outside bodies are undertaken for the Board of Trade from time to time: for example, a " measurement survey " was made recently to give guidance to manufacturers on the proportion of different sizes of clothing needed.

Make-do and Mend

Investigation of needs has been accompanied by a carefully worked-out scheme for helping people to make the best use of the garments they already possess. The Make-do and Mend campaign is designed not merely to revive the lost arts of darning and patching, but to raise morale by showing how old clothes can be turned into really smart and attractive new ones. A small staff at the Board of Trade co-operates with officials of the Ministry of Education, with Local Education Authorities, and with the Women's Voluntary Organisations all over the country, and to-day some 50,000 Make-do and Mend classes are meeting regularly. Hundreds of exhibitions have been held, varying from small shows in village halls to an elaborate display in a famous London store, but always with exhibits—of a steadily rising standard of taste and quality—made by ordinary members of Make-do and Mend classes. Many retail shops now hold regular displays and exhibitions, while others provide space for advice centres where the busy woman can consult experts not only on the problem of dress but on methods of repairing all kinds of household equipment. Exhibitions have been staged in factories, and advice centres opened in canteens where workers can get information during the lunch break, while in some factory canteens classes are held after working hours. For those unable to attend classes, regular advertising of the achievements of "Mrs. Sew-and-Sew" appear in both newspapers and women's magazines, and the Board of Trade's booklet of hints and instructions is a steady best-seller, with over 1½ million copies sold.

CHAPTER VI

Furniture and Household Goods

ALTHOUGH the Limitation of Supplies Orders began to restrict manufacture of many types of household goods within a few months of the outbreak of war, stocks were so large that it was not until 1941 that a general and widespread shortage began to be felt by consumers. In the summer of 1940 many thousands of housewives responded to the appeal of Lord Beaverbrook, then Minister of Aircraft Production, to give their aluminium saucepans to be melted down for use by the aircraft industry, and at that time it was possible to find substitutes for the articles sacrificed without any serious difficulty. A year later, however, restrictions on production had noticeably affected supplies in the shops, while the need to conserve materials and to release labour and factory space for other purposes resulted in the introduction of further restrictions. At the same time, the heavy bombing of the winter of 1940–41 had increased the normal demand for articles of everyday use.

The most serious shortage was in the supply of furniture, and a general welcome was given to the announcement of the President of the Board of Trade, made in August 1942, that he had decided to appoint a committee to advise him on the design and production of "utility" furniture. The vice-president of the Council for Art and Industry was appointed chairman, and the members included both experts on furniture production and men and women with a close knowledge of the needs of the average householder. Within two months an exhibition of the selected designs was being held in London and plans for distribution were already so far advanced that it was possible to announce that the scheme would come into operation in January 1943.

The plan thus devised had a three-fold object: first, to secure the utmost economy in the use of labour and materials; secondly, to ensure that in circumstances of extreme scarcity furniture should be made available to those whose need was greatest; and, thirdly, to make possible a satisfactory system of price control.

The manufacture of furniture to other than utility specifications was prohibited, and the manufacture of utility furniture undertaken by firms selected by the Board of Trade after careful consideration of their geographical location, the labour supply position in the different areas, and the production facilities and types of production normally engaged in by different firms. Regular contact between the Board of Trade and the Trade Associations covering the different branches of the industry ensures the smooth working of the scheme and makes it easy to iron out difficulties as soon as they arise.

The designs chosen by the advisory committee are simple and modern, and extraordinarily pleasing. The need for economy has eliminated all unnecessary elaboration, and has reduced the number of designs to the minimum required to meet the needs of homes of varying types. It has also involved the disappearance of such comfortable pieces of furniture as deep-sprung armchairs and the conventional three-piece suite of two armchairs and a settee—a sacrifice made necessary by the shortage of springs and other materials needed for upholstery. On the other hand, many of the articles are in the best tradition of English furniture-making: thus, one of the tables is based on the design of an eighteenth-century card-table, with a top which swings round and opens to double its original width, disclosing a sizable storage space underneath for knives and forks, table linen and mats. There is an easy-chair which unfolds into a single bed and which is taken from a design originally produced by William Morris, one of the most remarkable of all

English designers of furniture, at the end of the last century; and one of the chairs is a modification of the Windsor chair, which has been at home in British kitchens for many hundreds of years. Such designs as these are easy to live with, well adapted to their job, and have a grace, and sometimes even a distinction, seldom associated with the cheaper grades of furniture where mass-production has in the past been masked with mass-produced carving and other decorations that were often as hideous as they were unnecessary. There is no doubt at all that utility production has done much to raise the standard of furniture design, and some manufacturers are already anticipating that when it is possible to produce these and similar designs in materials of good quality there will be a big demand for them, not only in the home market but also abroad.

Scarcity of Wood and Materials

Unfortunately, but inevitably, the standard of quality in materials has not always been worthy of the design. The shortage of wood has made it necessary to use hardboard, made from wood fibre, thinly veneered with wood on both sides, for panels of cupboards and shelves and drawers, and though as a substitute material hardboard is reasonably satisfactory, it obviously will not stand up to the wear and tear of a long lifetime. On the whole, however, the difficult problem of finding suitable materials in a period of acute shortage has been tackled with considerable and growing success.

The great scarcity of materials has also made it necessary to restrict the sale of utility furniture to those whose need is most urgent, and a stringent, but very ingenious, system of rationing has been adopted. Such furniture may only be bought by those who fall within certain clearly defined categories, known as priority classes: first come those whose homes have been bombed, then those setting up house for the first time either because they have young children or because a child is expected; next comes the claim of couples married since the war and couples who propose to marry and set up house within three months of making an application for a permit to buy furniture, and, finally, people who need a bed for a growing child. Each applicant, after he has satisfied the authorities that he does in fact fall within one of these categories, is issued with a certain number of buying units. Each article of furniture is valued at a fixed number of units, and the purchaser is then free to spend his units on those articles of which he is most urgently in need. The choice can be made either by study of a published catalogue or by examining sample furniture at a retail store, which then places the orders. The maximum number of buying units granted to any applicant is not more than sufficient to provide the most essential items, and even for these the purchaser must be prepared to wait several months for delivery, while difficulties in the supply position have made it necessary to defer the buyer's right to " cash "—or, rather, exchange for furniture—more than a proportion of his units. Delays, however, have seldom been so prolonged as to lead to complaints from would-be buyers, and during the latter part of 1944 there was a substantial easing of the position. Cots, play-pens and chairs suitable for very young children are sold without restriction, and a recent concession has provided that people entitled to buy utility furniture may also buy a certain quantity of curtain material without the surrender of clothing coupons, which are normally required from purchasers.

All prices are fixed, and the combined effect of controlling prices and removing purchase tax from utility furniture has meant that few, if any, would-be purchasers are deterred by the cost; indeed, the general level of prices is remarkably low.

Improvement in Public Taste

There can be no doubt that the success of the scheme has been remarkable, both in effecting big savings in labour, materials and factory space, and in ensuring a distribution which is widely applauded for its fairness. More surprising is the fact that, as with utility clothing, the need for economy has been turned to definite and positive advantage by designers, and that there has been a real, and no doubt permanent, rise in the standard of public taste. When it is possible to release scarce materials and to allow a wider variety of design and a greater freedom to buy, the tradition already established should prove of great value to manufacturers and purchasers alike, and in this connection it is interesting to note that the President of the Board of Trade has recently set up an expert committee to advise on the design and character of domestic and other furniture during the immediate post-war period.

The success of utility clothing and furniture has led to the application of similar principles to the production of a wide variety of other articles. Towels, which, to the regret of all housewives, are only to be bought in exchange for the surrender of clothing coupons, were brought within the field of utility production along with sheets and other household linens. The utility range is of excellent quality, and prices are often only a third or a quarter of those asked for comparable articles outside the scheme. Soft bedding, pillows, quilts and mattresses are all now made to utility specifications, and though supplies are not large, the persistent housewife can generally, if with a little difficulty, find, within the range of her purse, the articles of which she is most in need.

Concentration of production, described in a previous chapter, has greatly restricted the output not only of textiles but of all types of household goods, and people who have lost their homes, or who are setting up house for the first time, find it far from easy to obtain many types of domestic equipment that were taken for granted, at least in the more comfortable homes, in pre-war days. Vacuum-cleaners, refrigerators and such useful gadgets as electric toasters and coffee percolators are no longer made, with the result that the advertising columns of newspapers and magazines carry long lists of people anxious to buy, or willing to sell, second-hand household goods. Similarly, many of the big stores have opened departments for the sale of second-hand household linens and china as well as furniture of all kinds. Saucepans, kettles and other types of hard-ware for the kitchen are still being made, though it is not always easy to find them in the shops, and the quality—again because of the shortage of materials—is much below that of pre-war days, while prices are high.

China and pottery are also extremely scarce, though the production of utility pottery has made it possible to obtain the most essential utensils without much difficulty; but restrictions on the use of colour and the increasing coarseness of the materials used has meant that utility pottery, unlike many other types of utility production, has no other advantages than those which its name implies—it is useful, reasonably priced, though not of a design calculated to arouse any particular pride in its possession. But in this field, too, the housewife realises that the utility scheme has helped to ease her problems, and, in fact, consumers frequently express the wish that the field covered by utility production might be widened still further.

In this connection, reference must be made to two branches of utility production that fall outside the ordinary domestic sphere, namely, pencils and automatic lighters. Utility pencils are now the only pencils produced, and while they lack the finish of pre-war pencils (they are of plain wood, without paint or varnish) the quality is good and prices are low. Similarly, the production of automatic cigarette lighters is now confined to utility models sold at a uniform, and low, price. Supplies are plentiful and the utility lighter, though inferior to the typical automatic lighter of pre-war days, is a neat, well-designed substitute which, partly because of the acute shortage of matches, is widely popular.

CHAPTER VII

Consumers and Producers

CONTROL over consumption has added enormously to the responsibilities of the housewife. Previous chapters have described the various limitations on her freedom to buy where and what—within the limits of her income—she likes. Other restrictions limited her opportunities still further: the black-out and risks of air raids shortened the hours during which shops were open. Retailers' deliveries of all commodities other than bread and milk were allowed to be made only once a week. A scheme to save labour and other costs in milk distribution allows only one dairy to deliver in any one street, and from this the housewife must take her milk or else herself collect it from the shop. (The only exception to this regulation is that those who in peacetime were members of co-operative societies are not obliged to transfer their custom to private traders.) Those who wish to buy the scarcer foodstuffs, such as fish and fruit and, in some districts, cakes and pastries, must still shop early and be prepared to stand in a queue and then to run the risk of coming away unsatisfied.

Her shopping done, the average housewife still has before her a heavy programme of cooking, house-cleaning and mending that demands from her the maximum of skill in using unfamiliar or scarce ingredients and in making do with equipment growing daily more dilapidated. The woman who before the war kept one or two servants now usually has none, and millions of women who once found their domestic duties a full-time job have been doing important work outside the home. More than three million married women have been engaged in paid employment, millions of others undertook civil defence duties or other part-time voluntary work, while others again had evacuated children or transferred war-workers billeted on them. In many parts of the country, but especially in London and the south, air raids and V-weapons added to the general sense of strain.

In these circumstances it would not be surprising if the relaxation of wartime restrictions were anticipated with exaggerated hope. Some people urge that increases in food rations should be postponed until the needs of our Allies in Europe can be satisfied; many fear that a post-war boom will be followed by another great slump; and all are determined that the many lessons learned under the stress of war shall not be forgotten in days of peace.

Employment policy is eagerly debated. The Coalition Government's proposals, around which controversy centred, included plans for control over the location of industry and for a re-allocation of workers from war industries to those whose output will be most vital to the reconstruction programme. The depressed areas of the inter-war years were to be developed as Reconstruction Areas, and the President of the Board of Trade announced that in these areas a number of new factories of the most modern design had already been completed and would be able to go into production as soon as the demand for munitions relaxed sufficiently to make available labour and raw materials. Other factories built for munitions production have, it has already been pointed out, added substantially to Britain's industrial potential. New industrial processes, developed under the stress of war, can be adapted to peacetime uses, and with the diminution of the demand for new types of weapons, designers have begun to plan for the needs of consumers both at home and abroad. Recent exhibitions of models to be used in post-war housing—both permanent and temporary—have set a new standard in the design of some important items of domestic equipment, and an important development has been the adaptation of methods used in aircraft construction to the building of houses and flats. In furniture and clothing, wartime designs have notably raised the level of public taste, while the need to economise in the use of labour has stimulated productive efficiency.

Indeed, in spite of the call-up of skilled men to the Forces, there can be no doubt that the war has increased the skill and adaptability of British labour. Training centres, some run by the Ministry of Labour and others by employers for their own work-people, have shown how quickly a man or woman of normal intelligence can be taught to perform intricate and delicate processes. And while the need for mass-production has brought about big advances in methods of factory organisation, the traditional skill of the British worker has been sharpened by his experience in handling new tools and unfamiliar materials. At the same time, the worker's interest in his job has often been stimulated by the setting up of Joint Production Committees at which representatives of the management and workers in war factories discuss methods of eliminating waste and increasing efficiency.

These committees, together with such other types of democratic control as local Food Control Committees and the various advisory committees set up by different Government Departments, have given the ordinary citizen a sharpened awareness of his responsibilities. Democracy in wartime has not merely preserved the citizen's right to grumble—a right which has been exercised with a moderation that has flowed from his understanding of the need for restrictions—but it has made him more clearly aware of his duty to see for himself that when things go wrong he himself should do something to see that they are put right. The fashion for " brains trusts " and a lively spate of political pamphleteering are indications that, in spite of long hours of tedious work and the growing complexity of Government regulations, democracy has acquired a new vigour, while the circumstances of war—both in the call-up of men and women to industry and the Forces and in the adoption of rationing and the controlled distribution of supplies—have produced a new sense of social equality.

There have been many hardships, and not all of them have come to an end with the cessation of hostilities. But the gains to be set against the vast sum of suffering and loss are not inconsiderable. In industry, those whose task is to plan for the post-war period have learned much that should be of immense value in helping Britain to play a significant part in the economic reconstruction of Europe and the enrichment of the world.

eat
Daily
greens
FOR HEALTH
FEED RIGHT
TO FEEL RIGHT

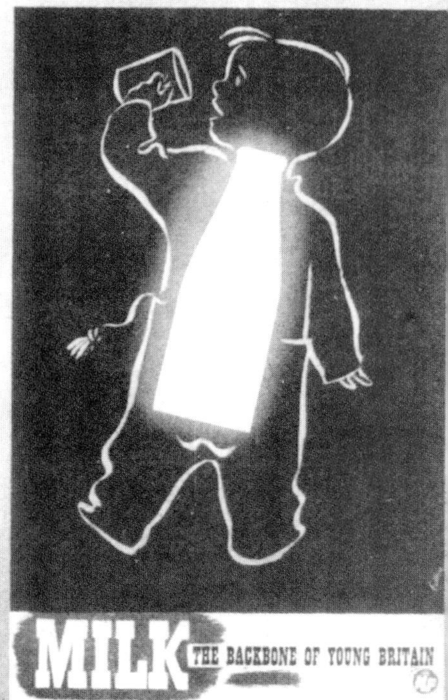
MILK
THE BACKBONE OF YOUNG BRITAIN

If you didn't want it
why did you take it
?

The right way
to cook greens
LID ON TIGHTLY TO KEEP THE STEAM IN
A CUPFUL OF BOILING WATER OR JUST ENOUGH TO KEEP THE PAN FROM BURNING
GREENS SHREDDED BEFORE COOKING
Cook for 10 minutes, or 15
– if the greens are tough

THINK AHEAD
write instead
TELEGRAPH AND TELEPHONE LESS

"PERHAPS THIS'LL TEACH YOU TO
STAY AT 'OME NEXT 'OLIDAY"